careless blossoming

Careless Blossoming, a brilliant new collection of poems by Lana Maree Haas, is structured in 4 thematically grouped sections: "seeds," "softness," "scent," and "wild cold." We experience through them the seasons of the planet, the stages of physical life, rituals of birth and rebirth, of connection and loss, and an awareness of our perfect and timeless true nature, an ecstatic dance that Lana repeatedly invites us to join. "Are You Coming with Me?" she asks.

There is also a sacredness so holy and personal that it is ineffable, as in the first lines we read in the opening section: "there is pure music / that I haven't sung for you / there are secrets / that I hold inside / just for me." We are reminded of the innocence with which we entered the world, and that is still accessible to us, as in "Everyone Listen with Star Eyes": "I am a child / I listen with star eyes." We are also reminded that the innocent child has nothing to fear when faced with the ephemeral nature of our worldly existence: "Do Like I Do": "if you don't know what to do / when the clock strikes that last hour / just do like I do / and love as far as your heart / allows." Love fully embraced leaves no room for doubt or anxiety.

There is also a mature understanding of what elements of life lead to an experience of wholeness, and an impatience with distracting meaningless chatter. In "All or Nothing" we are told "don't speak / unless the sounds / lead to freedom"... "don't whisper in my ear / unless the touch / leads to union." In other poems a transcendental darkness becomes the mysterious cloaked time of "Night Bliss:" "hello beautiful / darkest night of mine / I am drowning in the pleasure / of knowing you"... "I am delighted at the treasures / bestowed by you."

A desire to be one with The Beloved is a constant theme, and the enjoyment of earthly sensuality is part of the wave that lifts us to higher consciousness and renews our awareness of the ecstatic spark, the thrill of being alive in this present moment. In "Blue Resuscitation" we read "give me a gift / of blue iridescence"... "drape it around my neck / and I will lean in / while you bestow / a kiss that heals my veins." In "Desiderate" there is a shifting sense of inner and outer: "I would kiss you in sleep and in dreams / I would wake up to your almost arms / and hands / caressing my hair"... "my eyes softening"... "I would sing a morning hum so quietly"... "that only you would hear"... "a note / a lover's tune / a longing for you."

All of this is achieved with a brevity of language that is drawn from air and light, the sounds of drums and dancing, breath and heartbeat, and soft moments of stillness laden with stars. In "the wild cold," as we face the inevitability of our departure from this plane, we are given confidence that all is unfolding perfectly, as in "Redemption," where our moment of dread is quickly subsumed in liquid language that moves joyfully toward holy union: "we will flow like water"... "and at the edge of time / at the end of the path / we'll dread the drop to certain death / and spread our wings so wide / and let the breath of God lift us."

This little commentary only hints at the richness of this collection. It is an affirmation of life, love, beauty, and the fullness of human experience which I hope finds its rightful place in the hearts and homes of many. May your lives be blessed by Lana's superbly crafted poems, as has mine.

— **JOHN GREENLEAF-MAPLE**, B.A., English/Creative Writing, author, teacher, artist and poet careless blossoming

careless blossoming

POEMS BY
LANA MAREE HAAS

2022
GOLDEN DRAGONFLY PRESS

FIRST PRINT EDITION, March 2022
FIRST EBOOK EDITION, March 2022

Copyright © 2022 by Lana Maree Haas
All rights reserved.

Edited by Tammy Stone
Cover art by Tim Behrens
Cover photograph by Desiree Pratt
Layout by Alice Maldonado
Set in Sabon LT Pro and Calluna

No part of this publication may be reproduced or transmitted in any form or by any means, electronic or otherwise, without prior written permission by the copyright owner.

ISBN-13: 978-1-7370545-0-4

Library of Congress Control Number: 2021952254

Printed on acid-free paper supplied by a Forest Stewardship Council-certified provider. First published in the United States of America by Golden Dragonfly Press, 2022.

www.goldendragonflypress.com

*There are days we live
as if death were nowhere
in the background; from joy
to joy to joy, from wing to wing,
from blossom to blossom to
impossible blossom, to sweet impossible blossom.*

— L<small>I</small>-Y<small>OUNG</small> L<small>EE</small>

I want to dedicate this book to all of my friends and family who have nudged, encouraged and inspired me to write it.

And to my children, Miranda and Desiree, who have added infinite beauty to my soul and given me reasons to dream.

contents

Acknowledgments	xv

seeds

Everyone Listen with Star Eyes	4
Guardians of the Night	6
Wounded Healer	7
Love Letter to My Friends	9
True Blue	10
Jupiter	11
Ever-arriving Living Undying	13
Beating on a Drum Drumming	14
Bird Sings My Heart Open	16
Do Like I Do	17
Possibilities	19
All or Nothing	21
Are You Coming with Me?	22

softness

The Medicine We Need	26
You Are Allowed	27
Visitation	28
For Reed	29
After Thoughts	30
Why Be Jealous?	33
How We Forgive	35

Today	36
Body Is Still	37
Midsummer Moment	38
The Long Shadow Day	39
The Moon and the Mother	40
Dissolution of a Nation	42

scent

Orange Blossom Honey	46
Water	48
Listen	49
Alchemist	51
I Saw You in a Dream	52
Samhain	53
Endless Reasons to Go Barefoot	54
A Bargain	55
Chasing Freedom	56
Firekeeper	57
Ecstatic Dance Me!	58
Moon Swoon	60
Blue Resuscitation	61
A Woman Wilding	63
Night Bliss	66
Desiderate	67
Sun Man	68
Trust	69
Wind Answers	70
Iris	71

wild cold

The Sky on the Upswing	77
Redemption	79
Contraction	80
The Radiant Map of My Living Heart	81
Outbreath	83
Friday Night	84
Time Warp	85
We Were	86
The Whole Picture	87
Have Spring	89
Path of Healing	90
Our Beloved Aaron	92
Paralysis	94
Isolation	95
I Do Not Disappear	98
About Lana	101

Acknowledgments

GRATEFUL ACKNOWLEDGMENT goes out to the editors of the publications in which a few poems from this book first appeared. "Listen" and "The Radiant Map of My Living Radiant Heart" and "You Are Allowed" were first published in *Journey of the Heart: Women's Spiritual Poetry*, run by the talented and generous Catherine Schweig; "A Woman Wilding" first appeared in the anthology, *Goddess: When She Rules: Expressions by Contemporary Women*, edited by Catherine Schweig; and "Water" was published in *La Bloga*.

Endless thanks goes go out to Tammy Stone for her steadfast patience, praise and encouragement, and priceless help with editing my first book. It has been a beautiful and synchronistic flow of back and forth, and I am forever grateful for her keen eyes, ears, and heart in finishing this book.

I also owe much, much gratitude to Tim Behrens for his easygoing and flexible help, generosity, and talent in our many late night sessions on zoom designing the book cover. His cool, calm nature helped to ground me and his humor helped to lift me during this process.

Thank you to my daughter Desiree, who let me use her photo for the cover. It is perfect.

*all beings are blossoms
blossoming
in a blossoming universe*

— S<small>OEN</small> N<small>AKAGAWA</small>

seeds

there is pure music
I have not sung for you
there are secrets
I hold inside
just for me

Everyone Listen with Star Eyes

everyone listen

there are stars
that form
just for me

they drift down
to Earth
sometimes plummet!
they burn
they crash
into me!

they fill me up with the holiest
of holy light!
it is so much heaven
I cannot describe!

I birth them
as eyes
that see every
twinkling
bit of love
and ecstasy
looking into
and out of me
the forgotten reasons
I came into being
are ignited by star showers

that bless me
when I am
dreaming
awake
and
alive!

I am a child
I listen with star eyes

Guardians of the Night

we should
look at the moon rise
and hold hands
we should
sit in the darkening room
with the clock ticking silent dusk

trees black in the windows
our quiet comrades
our guardians of the night

we should
not forget
how little time
if any at all
we have left
to laugh and cry
to hold a hand in our own
and let the
nails on the coffin
of our past
be pushed out
by the swelling
of our soul's knowing

Wounded Healer

assume you're an angel
walking with death
stars protruding
from your ancient
fragile chest

assume your divinity
your beauty
your grace

questions on the path
drop in from the ethers
little planets of light
gifts for a queen

shake in happiness
wait for your arrival
hands and arms
endlessly embracing

fingers effervescent
touch the sky
above you

gather up the galaxies
like ribbons round a box

sing while you anticipate
communing with the moon
one last look is
forever comes too soon

assume you're an angel
wet tears of grief
glisten in your eyes
drop from your nose
your chin
your radiant shining cheeks

and fall into my hands
water
wind
and birth

assume you're an angel
walking with death
first and last
eternal opening
eternal truth

Love Letter to My Friends

dear friends
in the dark
we see by
a kind of light
it is not visible to the eye

unfurling in folds and crevices
in the fabric of life and time

where sight makes sound
and sound is silent

dear friends
we hold
each other near or far
in hearts that beat
in one knowing

be empowered
(however you are already divine)
be embodied
(however you are surely pure light)

in the dark we see
by that kind of light

True Blue

silky threads form
a blue-like light
the color of God
and the infinite sky
in my vision they dance
around my fingers
and through your bones

every moment
weaves a new
beginning
here is where
the healing is
and there it is too

asking me to pay
attention to
every breath
the smallest notice
the biggest blue
the pure one I know
the true you

Jupiter

there is some potent magic
in the night
if you focus your eyes
and walk outside
arms and hands free

then tilt your head
like the majestic planet
you are

and find yourself
in an open field
(or in the smallest clearing)
and stamp your feet
fearlessly on the ground

then look up
with eyes wide
and drop your

pre-economical
pre-historical
pre-fanatical
pre-philosophical
pre-factual
pre-conceptual
pre-vibrational
Pre-cortical
pre-technological

pre-scientifical
pre-pedagogical
pre-theosophical

notions

and see with a heart
and with a mind
echoing a home

the song you know
ringing out clearly
as the knower
who knows

Ever-arriving Living Undying

this new world is fraught with crystal clear thoughts that say:

1.
hold hands like undying springs

2.
reveal the precious nature of your true being

this new world blows in like a shaky wind
gentle to the tender
fierce to the rooted
and sure in purpose

gaze into the eyes of your beloved

she is ripe
she is ready
she is everywhere

come with your purest gifts
and open your flaming heart

new worlds are arriving every moment!

Beating on a Drum Drumming

beating on a drum drumming
why do I ever look out
instead of looking in?

beating on a drum
drumming

the sound
the mother

beating on a drum
how do I hope to win?
all the endings
all the beginnings

beating on a drum
drumming

my soul the flower
this dance
this hour

beating on a drum
my watch
my witnessing
no flinching
no blinking

beating on a drum
drumming

why do I ever look out
instead of looking in?
beating on a drum
drumming
all heart
no thinking

beating on a drum
drumming

all the endings
all the beginnings

Bird Sings My Heart Open

twilight sang ahead
of the day
when I was happy
and playing

I forgot
to say your name
I forgot the sound
of your voice

and then a bird
sang my heart open

and the sun
warmed my face

Do Like I Do

I guess we'll want to remember
the way the days were so slow
and time could be taken idly

I guess we'll want to remember
the way we lived
like little kings and queens
balancing and swinging
laughing and singing

and how we tore
the tumbling tower down
with our bare teeth and hands
blinded by a fierce light
never seeing and never looking

if you don't know what to do
when the clock strikes that last hour
just do like I do
and love as far as your heart
allows
and as wide as the ocean
that sits in your belly will hold
and as deep as the dark
tunnel of unknowing
takes its hold

fast forward in time
and we'll still be coming up

with poems and rhymes
in a little book of colors
scratching down the days
and remembering with wonder
how we got so close
to creating magic and beauty
in the ashes

throw all recollections
of our dying away now
scorching and drowning
into a pool of rare clear water
and watch stars being born

Possibilities

to touch you in a soft place
could take years
or a moment

could start an avalanche
or a firestorm

could make rising
flood waters raid the city
of pure awareness

or
it could grow a garden

to touch you in a soft place
could rearrange your physiology
your bones

or it might start
to shake you ferociously
with sounds that overwhelm you

like earthquakes
breaking our major faults
like thunder
rolling across the prairie
shifting winds and blowing grass seeds
like confetti

to touch you in a soft place
could be blinding like a flash of white light

or you could just miss it altogether

All or Nothing

don't speak
unless the sounds
lead to freedom

who wants to be trapped
in words and memories

don't whisper in my ear
unless the touch
leads to union

why open the holy grail
unless the kiss is real?

Are You Coming with Me?

if I breathe a deep enough breath
and the space is a cavernous waste
are you coming with me?

if I sing and the note is so high
our yearning ears deaf
to trumpeting angels in the sky
are you coming with me?

one finger tied to a thread
and I am whispering love notes
that cut diagonally in a live wire line
transcending fear and dread

my free fingers flying
vibrating a holy resonance
through my head

if I breathe a deep enough breath
are you coming with me?

softness

in the garden
sun and wind and birdsong
careless blossoming

The Medicine We Need

in the house of no walls
sky is heaven's ocean!
we breathe it all in
we breathe it all out

we know what's real
we know the heart
holds medicine for us all
and when the moment is ripe
the mystery unfolds

we pour our blessings
onto the Earth!
she's open and endless
she gives us new birth

she flows in rivers
mountains
streams and oceans
she blesses as we bless
she heeds as we heed
listening
creating
and singing
Earth's new opening!

the medicine we need

You Are Allowed

you are allowed to take a rest
to set your head upon your mother's breast
you are allowed the sweetest of sleep
to be near me
this close

you are allowed to lay your body down
near a river that sends bits of soft misty dew
dispersed in the air
to land upon your skin and soothe you

you are allowed to slip into nothingness
to listen only to silence and birds and gentleness
to forget anything that tugs at you
or torments you

you are allowed

you are so allowed the spaciousness you desire
and more
you are so allowed the forgiveness and acceptance
to free your mind and body from this mire

you are so allowed

Visitation

rainbows were coming
out of your mouth
speaking in elemental languages
while ancient prism tongues
danced along
the edge of an underground cave

singing velvet songs and sometimes
dipping down deep for a drink of

cool
clear
water

near the cave-tops
convexed inside
a bowl of glistening light
molten messages
encoded in thousands of tiny droplets
each reflecting the song you sang to me
when yesterday danced around our heads
lighting us alive in green sacred geometry

For Reed

transparent notes
float above the water
and sing a song in sunlight setting

remembering you
in silence
when yesterday your feet walked here
among us

among giants
living trees stood before us
awakened by your radiance

here we witnessed
your tender beauty

After Thoughts

I wanted to say

the other day

under the Earth
below my feet

beneath the concrete

how there are tremors

tiny electrons
magnetic bliss

I waited to say it on this day
because I am in ecstasy

I want you to know
how the shaking
and the movement
are unraveling me

waking me

like a lover who envelopes me

arms entwined around me
dancing
and spinning me

I wanted to say

how I love you until forever
right now

I waited to say it
because I didn't want to hear you say

"don't be trite now"

but now I am spinning
silently singing your name
and it's my name too

I wanted to ask you
the other day

if trees just allow the sway
or is it just the wind
having her way?

this love is complete right now
this love is perfect right now

I wanted to say
how I waited to this day
because I am turning
and orbiting

being pulled fervently into harmony
and blessed purpose

saving nothing and everything

racing through space in total ecstasy

I wanted to say how
birds and trees and skies and planets

know infinity

just like you and me

Why Be Jealous?

you are rain
so why be jealous
of words
of a glance
just be
remembering me
like drops of quiet listening

you are my skin
you are recycling in me
in radiant descending
and rising

little scratched knees
falling into playfulness
on the cement
on the grass
green painted bliss

you are magic
and mine always
you are my soul
and my deepest love
beloved teacher
residing in me

you are held here
in my delicate cupped hands
embraced by a bow

bowing again
and again
love in a vessel
in a body
like mine

How We Forgive

how do we forgive
our transgressions
locked in solid ice
too hard to remember?

how do we forgive
our forgetfulness
the fog
and the hairline fractures?

how do we let go
of the tension
of the stretching
and the seeking
for more and more detail
in an effort to rescue
a small wind
that carries the message

she is a breeze blowing through
our hair and our hands
that whispers the answers
on our faces
and in our hearts

how do we listen
to that?

Today

today my poem
is personal

filled with ache
and a longing

so tender
and hurting

no answers
but a wish

and a letting go
because I must

today my poem
is personal

because I cannot
show you

the very center
of my heart

today
my words
won't be adequate
to convey to you

how I am human
and how I loved you

Body Is Still

body is still
breathing in
through lips so full
of kissing blissful air
body is still
breathing out
body's holy light

body is still
waters calm
buoyant blessing
deep caressing

body is still
healing hearts
come and go
meet and part

body is still
one heartbeat
beating on
one beats after one
until there are none

body is still
nothing space
nothing time
can erase

Midsummer Moment

this extended moment
opens my heart
in suspended longing
on a planet spinning
to the sounds of

blades of grass
blowing in winds of rapture
dripping with dewdrops
and silent fireflies
blinking in and out

ever-slowing
quiet pausing
light extending
never-ending

The Long Shadow Day

I sink into a corner

of the living room
where friendly spirits
sit with me

and the long shadow day
reminds me of the cold that waits
and may arrive tomorrow
or in January

I cannot
or won't
rise from the corner
where my cheeks are humming and warm
sunk into
happily solid
and stuck in the cushion

a rare day of nothing
but fresh air blowing
through the windows
in autumn

The Moon and the Mother

pretty soon
I will need you to be
the moon
and the mother

pretty soon
our heads will form
the halos we deserve

quietly reflecting
fervently reaching
asking for repentance
bowing in acceptance
receiving our rightness

pretty soon
you'll be asking
what next?
and you'll look out
and see a great need
and hands
that beg to be held

pretty soon   I love you

pretty soon   always holding you

pretty soon
a young mother
will hold her swelling belly

rocking and soothing you
pretty soon
I will need you to be
the moon
and the mother

the hand holder
and the tear wiper

and you will grace the planet
with songs
and healing laughter

pretty soon
I will need you to be
the moon
and the mother

pretty soon
you will look out and see in
you will know
what you came here for
and where you begin

pretty soon
nothing will look familiar

don't worry then
call out my name
I will find you

like only a mother can

Dissolution of a Nation

this flag of nations
people and boundaries
marks the entrance
to the watery graves
of the ancients
and the lonely howls
of souls forgotten

this flag is like a wing
a feather and a prayer
that I will consume
and burn in my fiery heart

this flag doesn't exist
this flag is nowhere

instead my hands
touch your arm
your face
your chest

in that moment
you can let go
of anything you resist
and breathe
into my loving openness

scent

love in a bottle
wind and perfume
all the flavors
taste like you

Orange Blossom Honey

if I could
I would put a drop of
orange blossom honey
in your mouth
and let it find its way
into your heart
to soothe your
worrying
and your lonely doubts

if I could
I would climb
your mountains
and bring you
a sign of hope
from under the snow
a little promise
like a rainbow
reflected in a snowflake
or the first sign
of spring
melting

if I could
I would make
everything alright

but I don't know anything
about the way you breathe

or curl up and weep
when no one can see

if I could
I would take
this pain from you
but then
you'd never know
or receive the gift
you've been dying
to open yourself up to

and so I am loving you

if I could
I would
show you
the beauty of you
and how easy
it is to love you
and you'd see what I mean
seen from the eyes of me
knowing you

how beauty lives in you
how easy it is to love you

Water

I saw you in the river
when ripples of green
were humming and singing
unencumbered and laughing!
I knew it was you
because when I knelt to touch you
my fingers were blessed
and my face was caressed

Listen

listen
shall we create beauty today
like trees do
in the root and the sway?

shall we dance like stars tonight
so distant
so far
so real and surreal
landing in our feet
and pulsing in our heart

shall we create the cosmos
and the luminous bodies?
the moonbeams?
the galaxy?
moving in some ethereal quality

unreachable
unteachable
crescendoing cacophony?

booming!
bursting!
blossoms!

silent radiant bombshells
opening to penetrating sunbeams
unfathomable creations of beauty!

flowers   flowering
gracefully   posing

shall we listen to them opening and closing?

Alchemist

because I sit
with demons
and talk to angels
laughing

because I dance
with fervor
and abandon

because I love
so completely

because I
can be me

I Saw You in a Dream

I saw you in a dream

with your hair spilling down
your back
ringlets
wild as the river
hands in the mud

a faint call of geese
less than organized
broken V's
trying to regroup

and my knees
dance
the wolf in me

while your
slow motion shaman
soothes me

my spine moves
underwater
like dolphins
laughing

and sweet
benevolent raven
– a crazy genius for
LOVE!

I saw you in a dream

Samhain

I crave a wide open space
that leads to a forest floor
with autumn-colored leaves
to cover my face
and paths to traverse
that only I see
soiley pad underfoot
crunchy with the fallen
speaking in
an echoing tone
ancestor bones
walking me home

Endless Reasons to Go Barefoot

I smell the wildness in the dirt
walking on the soft Earth
where my lovely toes caress

they know

I smell the scent of want and hurt
I look with keen observe

and reserve

endless reasons to go barefoot
mining jewels in the interim

A Bargain

trade all of your books
to stand under the dark moon
while the sun seeks shadow

listen to the night calls
the clicking
the chirping
the singing
the howling
as silent wings glide
through cool air

and look in the dark
for nothing but your
beloved
listening to the whistling
the whispering
the leafless wintering

trade all of your noise and nonsense

all of it

for a deep kiss
and a knowing

Chasing Freedom

I chased a soaring bird
through thorny forest floors
and rocky ridges filled with
streaming mountain waters

I followed her through the valley
and ran underneath
her shadow lengthening...

she screeched long and high
and echoes from the land
answered
filling my whole being
proclaiming:

here is the wide wide sky!
the running waters!
and the majestic mountains!

Firekeeper

look

I've become water
with my hands raised up
to receive the unseeable
while my feet fan flames
that reach up from the ground

look

I've driven a stake into the ground
only to find all of the others
missing

the wind blows my shelter sideways

so I dig a hole with a silver spade
and open my mouth to pour in a blessing

underground
so many sleepers light up
when they hear the sound

look

it's not me or you
but something else
that ignites the night

Ecstatic Dance Me!

when I take a bow
this kind of music
sways me
to the beat of the
unknown
the ecstatic
ocean
waves
me!

the rose
the thorn
the underground
the sun shines
me!

all colors
remind me
a dip
a crest
a movement
feet
tap
slide
bounce
back
and
forth
me!

when I take a bow
this kind of beat
slays me
hips
breasts
arms
knees
under
all around
ecstatically
propelling
me!

over
all
above
the trancing
takes shape
in forms
that move
inside
and
outside
me!

synapses
electricity
ecstatically
dancing
me!

Moon Swoon

I don't call you moon
for any particular reason
and I won't call you long distance
when you are within reach

drop down into my lap
and sink your heavy lamp
into my thighs
rest your unevenness
in one deep peaceful breath

I am strong enough to survive
the buoy of birth
and the weight of death

Blue Resuscitation

give me a gift
of blue iridescence
the kind that rests on my heart
and moves with my rhythmic chest

drape it around my neck
and I will lean in
while you bestow
a kiss that heals my veins
your precision
your intention
so delicate

your fingers hold smoke
and sparks
and tuning forks
they rattle the gates
and loosen the locks

give me the gift of a blue gem

so smooth and round
so perfectly polished
so perfectly weighted and sound

I'll wear it into the darkness
into alleys and forests
I'll wear it in the places

I call home and creation
I'll wear it in the sun
and lay it at my altar
and rest my body here
in blue resuscitation

and in my belly
where music holds its station
rising up from a heat
and a crystal clear river
she will infuse the softest
parts of me
with the voice of blue lapis
and the song of my blue planet

A Woman Wilding

old and stale
breathing shale
sloughing off
heartbeat tales

dancing on the grieving floor

find a rhythm
find a step
regale the waking sounds
and let them fall
a steady sprawl
loosened down
upon the shaking ground!

there is more!
there is more!

dancing on the grieving floor!

she can feel me
she's my sanctuary
when all of my anger
and my steady hallow grief
becomes a crying naked noise
breathing in
the stabbing past
spewing out
the acrid ash

shall I be all that?
where's the room
for a woman gone mad?

there is more!
there is more!
dancing on the grieving floor!

raging in a dance!

shaking in a trance!

a pining pitching fervor
a rumbling messy murmur
where do I stand
when I've lost my place?
my true north has no say!

there is more!
there is more!
dancing on the grieving floor!

I flail and I flaunt
without a thought
and she accepts
and celebrates!
movements big or small
smooth or jerky
sensual or smart
spent or wanting

there is more!
there is more!
dancing on the grieving floor!

I am bleeding tears into her
ample chest

I am melting skin and
diamond sweat

I am turning into flowing
flood waters
fists and fingers claw the
shattered altar

dancing like a woman wilding!

shall I be all that?
where's the room for
a woman gone mad?

there is more!
there is more!
dancing on the grieving floor!

Night Bliss

hello night
darkest night

I am so deep
deep in love with you

hello night
all dressed up
with lights for eyes
and a shiny cloak
of deepest colors

in my hands an overflowing cup
a drink to nature's cadence

hello beautiful
darkest night of mine
I am drowning in the pleasure
of knowing you

I am delighted at the treasures
bestowed by you

Desiderate

I would kiss you in sleep and in dreams
I would wake up to your almost arms
and hands
caressing my hair

my eyes softening

I would sing a morning hum so quietly
that only you would hear

I would whisper in your ear
I would move in you
I would rock in your embrace
and be consumed by your salty taste

and that quiet hum would be on my tongue
a note
a lover's tune
a longing for you

Sun Man

my sun man
one day thinks he's nothing
one day thinks he's all of it

my sun man
blinded by
a sudden light
he can't describe

makes him
wobble with
the force of
a million
rays
of
pure
love
lit

never did he
ever see
a light
as bright
as me

Trust

I tipped my toes on a tightrope
above the pink clouds
where below
lay
mystery

wobbling but
balanced
screaming
when falling

through
misty nothing
laced with
rose-colored dust

my face a new hue
your lips
a new you

my trembling hands
cupped round my heart
opening that door

to let the
imminent
blazing
fire
eat
away the
nonsense

Wind Answers

how to do it
when the wind
has blown so hard
and not without
surprising me

I close my eyes
and in my visioning
there are magic
moving mountains
and dancing elk
going nowhere
along the edges
of time

Iris

you are particularly smitten
by a streak of charcoal ash
smeared across my cheek
unbeknownst to me

wild rises in the woods
in my thighs
the hook of glittering teeth
hungry for spring

my malleable psyche
my apprenticeship
embodied in a thousand lives
spread out before me

a banquet
an offering
heralding a dawn
of pure innocence

wild cold

moving curtains
fabric of snow
curling and dipping
rising and remembering

the sharp winter
the wild cold

The Sky on the Upswing

this is how I must be
like an urchin under the sea

with as little of my own movement
I can quiet the bones

with calcium and salt
I write the lines on my back
here I embed the codes
of the secrets we lack

with my electric hope
and fine-tuned fingers
I feel telling lines
and read the palms
of every lost soul

I feel the subtlety
the subliminal
and the rectifying
geometry
that lives like moving songs

and collects and distributes
reflects and deflects
unending creations

I become a vessel
and a speaker of silence

light is my song
I am captivated in utter stillness

I believe the sea when She speaks to me
in puckering salinity
lips smacking
my breath
pulsing
cooling and spiraling

I am mad with the upside down me
I can see the sky on the upswing
as the sea where I'm drowning

I see infinity
through tiny pinholes
flickering around you and me
in blue deep-sea listening

Redemption

we will walk forward
as if on a rolling sidewalk
no one will know if we are moving
one foot in front of the other
no one will know if we are standing still

we will walk so stealthily and readily

we will walk among the many
we will flow like water

and at the edge of time
at the end of the path
we'll dread the drop to certain death
and spread our wings so wide
and let the breath of God lift us

Contraction

I can still my breath
to an imperceptible
in
and
out

when I am holding
the grief inside

for what?

for
no
breathing
days like this

The Radiant Map of My Living Heart

it starts in a hut deep
in the winter woods
my feet on the ground
cold
fists shaking the air
frozen
sounds
mouth sounds howling
mist

woolen threads unravel me here

a small shelter
feathers and trinkets
sticks and mud

spinning blue pearls
unending stitching
on a map
radiant and glistening
beating and visceral
sacred knots and knowing vessels
each finger worn-round christened by a tear

each one held in a holy longing

by the in-pulsing
of the connection

of soul's longing
wilding running leaping

song

of my living radiant heart

it starts in a bed
made of rivers and rocking chairs

masts of sailboats gliding through glass
over ghosts and spirits
laying sleepy
nothing to grasp
and I am finally

now

here

forever moving towards the still point
where we collide

merging

in my living radiant heart

Outbreath

we are going to die first

we can hold our breath
we can puff our chests
we can lift our fists
we can furrow our brows
and look like this

we are going to die first

because we need a death
to make a new life

because we must leave
the whole of reality
and birth a new life

we are going to die first

so love gently
your true colors
your beaming heart
your pulsing radiance

a hundred million times
just like the ones we have already died
walking
flying
swimming
sighing

I am not afraid

Friday Night

in the streets of my town
surround sound
chittering messages

feet on pedals
roaring
bouncing
tires squeal

where I sit
where I am now

at the right lonely
moments
my charmed life

Time Warp

I could hear you talking
while the clock was ticking
behind me

over my shoulder
to the left
you were talking
to children
who hadn't
grown up
in cages

playfully dancing
in grass
with weeds
as friends

dragon snaps
for teacups
and rosebush
fortresses

I stand still
dreaming
that world alive
because
it was

no thoughts
no injustices
no world crumbling

no hearts
breaking

We Were

I was
you were
we were
the sun shining on
our every day

at least I remember
it that way

my arms
your eyes
there's our light

I say
you say
we never say
exactly
what we mean

and everything
golden that
I am
you are
we are

gets
misinterpreted
lost

The Whole Picture

I am air
in lungs
Earth
and a tongue
feet full
of mud
water
for fingers
I'm all and
nothing
I'm cold
and warm
hot lava
spewing
and the
small child
who hides
and
shakes

I'm joy
on a ride
I'm crying
inside
bumping
over rocks
and losing
bodily control

I'm a
handheld fan
in the heat
of summer
and the fear
of melding
myself
disappearing
into a lover

I'll hold your
hand through
some shit
saying
quiet
witnessing
heals
the wound

parts of me
come into
view

but
the whole
picture
waits
for you

Have Spring

have spring

without me

have that balmy wind
that inspires you
and sweeps out
our memories

seeds of all sorts
trembling
under your feet

awakening new

inspiring you
to hold someone's hand
like you did mine

and kiss her fully
like you did me
passionately

have spring

without me

Path of Healing

chaos
in a tunnel

I see nothing
I feel everything
dangerous
frightful
terrifying
and dank

and a voice speaking

listen and hear

here is your dark
here is your womb
and your abyss
here is the place
shaken from grace
deeper than space
darker than

the blackest
night

listen and hear

here are your very own demons
step in despite
your tremendous trembling

what awaits you is a death
and a holy remembering

it won't be easy
it won't be clear

listen and hear

here is the space
where secrets and unknowns
illuminated
become lost children forgiven
and broken hearts embraced

Our Beloved Aaron

this day
is teetering
on false
openings and closings
that lead
to lives
we
thought
we
were living

that sudden jolt
a crash!
your soul
free at last

this day
lingers
on
into
the next
like a waterfall
flowing upward
uncommon
unknown
and blessedly vexed

that lifting up

to the love that holds
us
deep and palpable
through shock
and grief
and gives us
something
to satisfy
our deepest need

this day
horrific
regrettable
untimely
unforgettable

this day
a light
a freeing
a lifting
a blessing

now holes in hearts
reverse in bloom
come together
in love for you
one last time to honor you
in the sweet and sacred
remembering room

Paralysis

how do

that's a question I won't

you

answer
honestly
for
fear of creating
more of

do

you

my fear
and unreality

do

unreal things that
grab me

you

my attention

Isolation

isolation 1

that train
that tornado
that tidal wave
it's coming
it's here

isolation 2

silent speaks loud and soft
fear and danger
hold still
don't breathe
don't touch
or hug me

isolation 3

sky is your home
Earth your mother
rain your redemption
sun your solace
I see my hands
now
same hands
but different

isolation 4

waiting
to hold a hand
to touch a face

waiting

holding my breath
take a breath in...
still shallow
incomplete

waiting

turning towards the wind
hair directionless and wild
beautiful danger

I Do Not Disappear

this happened
I opened
and then I closed

I did not disappear

this happened
for reasons undisclosed
and I did not disappear

each time
pain and an abyss
we all
in one way or another
know

when the cavern is wide
and the long fall begins
with body inverted
a chute
a tunnel
a dropping inside

that lingers
into drifting
into dark

while lost souls call
and reach out
for bits of skin

to eat and consume me
so they may live again
still the fall deepens
and I do not disappear

somewhere along the way
my flesh is frayed
caught on a rocky cliff
jagged knives and lips
will render any other direction futile

soul sounds silent
mouth is gone
words are null

and still
I do not disappear

stay present
remain wild in your nature
and
careless in your blossoming

About Lana

Photo by Ailecia Ruscin

LANA MAREE HAAS is a poet, songwriter, and sound healer living in the American Midwest. Her poetry has appeared in journals, including *Women's Spiritual Poetry*, *Rebelle Society*, *Women's Inc.*, and *LaBloga*, and in the anthology *Goddess: When She Rules: Expressions by Contemporary Women*.

She has also written, composed, and produced a solo album, *Stardust and Moonbeams*, and another album, *Riotous Singing!* with her band, The Sonic Mystics. One of her songs, "Peace and Harmony", appears on Snatam Kaur's album, *Sat Nam! Songs from Khalsa Youth Camp*.

She enjoys walking in forests, mountains, on beaches, and in the prairie with her dog Juno. She loves playing music with her friends and swimming in large bodies of water. This is her first poetry book.

Made in the USA
Middletown, DE
12 May 2022